LOOKING FOR LIFE
IN THE UNIVERSE

LOOKING FOR LIFE
IN THE UNIVERSE

THE SEARCH FOR EXTRATERRESTRIAL INTELLIGENCE

by Ellen Jackson

With photographs by Nic Bishop

Houghton Mifflin Company   Boston 2002

www.houghtonmifflinbooks.com

Book design by Lisa Diercks
The text of this book is set in FF Eureka
and House 3009 Spaceage Light and Vectagrams.

Endpapers: SETI uses the world's largest single-dish telescope at Arecibo in Puerto Rico to search for
evidence of extraterrestrial intelligence.
Facing title page: Many radio dishes linked together, similar to this array at Mt. Lassen in California, will
improve the search for extraterrestrial signals.

Additional image credits
Illustrations on pages 16, 17, 27, 37, and 46 by Nic Bishop. Images on pages 38 and 57 courtesy of
NASA/STSci. Image on page 39 provided courtesy of Malin Space Science Systems. For more
information, contact Malin Space Science Systems at www.msss.com. Image on page 40 courtesy of
NASA. Images courtesy of NASA/STSci have been incorporated in composite form on the front cover
and pages, 6, 26, 46, and 49. Images courtesy of NASA have been incorporated in composite form on
pages 16 and 37. Photographs on pages 28, 29, 30, 31, 32, and 33 courtesy of Jill Tarter.

Library of Congress Cataloging-in-Publication Data
Jackson, Ellen B., 1943–
Looking for life in the universe: the search for extraterrestrial intelligence / by Ellen Jackson ;
with photographs by Nic Bishop.
p. cm.
Summary: Investigates how scientists, particularly Jill Tarter, director for SETI at the SETI
Institute in Mountain View, California, use twenty-first-century technology to investigate whether
life exists on other planets.
ISBN 0-618-12894-8
1. Life on other planets—Juvenile literature. [1. Life on other planets. 2. Tarter, Jill C.
3. Scientists.] I. Bishop, Nic, 1955–   ill.
II. Title.
QB54.J22 2002
576.8'39—dc21   2001051312

Printed in Singapore
TWP 10 9 8 7 6 5 4 3 2 1

TO AMY FLYNN AND ANDREA BROWN,
    WITH THANKS
            —E.J.

CHAPTER ONE
IS SOMEBODY OUT THERE?

There was no other creature
That saw what I could see —
I stood and watched the evening star
As long as it watched me.
— SARAH TEASDALE

WE LIVE on an amazing planet, a planet filled with wonder and mystery. Seen from space, Earth is a blue-green jewel gleaming in the sky. No other planet in the solar system is home to apple trees, hummingbirds, and whales.

But could life exist elsewhere? Human beings have always looked at the heavens and asked: Are we alone? Are there other worlds or planets similar to Earth? Are these other planets inhabited by life—and what is that life like? Today scientists are using twenty-first-century technology to search for answers to these questions.

If living beings exist elsewhere in the universe, perhaps some of them are intelligent. They might have language. They might have something to say.

Many people believe in extraterrestrials, but scientists need evidence before they will accept a belief as true. Astrophysicists such as Jill Tarter, director for SETI at the SETI Institute in Mountain View, California, are looking for proof that intelligent life exists on other planets. The name SETI stands for Search for ExtraTerrestrial Intelligence.

Unfortunately, people can't actually travel to other solar systems. Even the closest stars are too far away to visit. A spaceship traveling at the speed of light would travel for more

The sun is about to rise on the world's largest radio telescope, at Arecibo in Puerto Rico. Cradled in a natural limestone depression, the vast dish can detect very faint radio signals from outer space.

than four years before reaching the nearest star, Proxima Centauri, which is 23.6 trillion miles (38 trillion kilometers) from Earth.

But scientists don't have to travel to other planets to look for life there. They can stay right here on Earth and search the sky for signals—signals from a civilization that uses radio transmissions or beams of light for interstellar communication. And that's exactly what SETI scientists do.

Twice a year at Arecibo, in the mountains of northwestern Puerto Rico, Jill Tarter and other members of the SETI Institute's Project Phoenix examine a few hundred sunlike stars using the world's largest radio telescope, an astonishing structure of aluminum and steel that looks like a suspension bridge dangling over a giant salad bowl. Jill and her team—Peter Backus, Mike Davis, Seth Shostak, Jane Jordan, John Ross, and others—spend most of their time overseeing the telescope, checking or fixing the computer equipment, and waiting for that first "hello" from outer space.

The control room used by the Project Phoenix astronomers gives no hint of the adventure of the SETI search. There are no panels of flashing lights, no panoramas of distant solar systems. Instead, three computer workstations, each with a monitor and keyboard, sit on tables along a wall. One workstation allows the scientists to observe where the telescope is pointing at a given time, which star is being examined, and the kinds of signals received. Another allows scientists to send and receive e-mail.

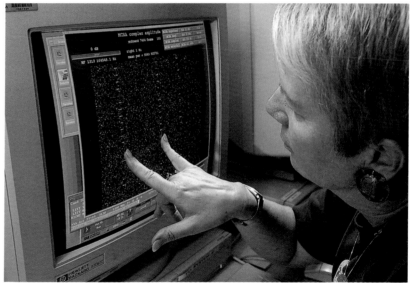

TOP: Signals received from the Arecibo dish are displayed on monitors in the control room.
BOTTOM: Jill examines a signal picked up by the dish, which later turned out to be interference from an Earth-bound source.

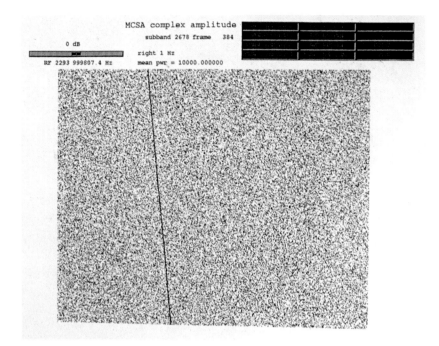

MCSA complex amplitude
subband 2678 frame   384
0 dB
right 1 Hz
RF 2293 999807.4 Hz   mean pwr = 10000.000000

The farthest detectable transmission from a human-made source, shown as a diagonal line on this data plot, comes from the tiny *Pioneer 10* spacecraft launched in 1972, which is now more than 7 billion miles from Earth.

The monitor of the third workstation displays a portion of the radio spectrum as a field of black and white dots. The white dots indicate high radio energy or noise—dark dots indicate low energy. A radio signal from an extraterrestrial source would show up as a slender line slicing through the salt-and-pepper background.

The diagonal line, usually seen by the team, comes from a human-made source, *Pioneer 10*, a spacecraft launched in 1972 to explore the outer planets of the solar system. *Pioneer 10* is now more than 7 billion miles from Earth, twice as far away from the sun as the planet Pluto. Although the transmitter on the spacecraft is very weak—giving off as much energy as a dim nightlight—the Arecibo telescope can usually detect it.

On this particular night, the SETI team is hard at work, checking out nearby star systems. Because the sun can distort radio signals, the team observes only after sunset, from six P.M. to six A.M.

Jill arrives a few minutes before midnight to begin her shift. Nearby, a large glass window reveals the night sky. Seen from the window, the Milky Way spans the horizon like a pale river of light. A mechanical chirp can be heard as the telescope moves slightly to adjust for Earth's rotation. It is following one tiny pinprick in this mighty stream of stars.

Before sitting down, Jill puts on a CD of Latin jazz and does a little dance around the room. Jill loves to dance. Then she hangs the Flag of Earth on the wall behind the computer monitors. It will remain hanging until the team finishes their work.

"People are so concerned about whether others are black or white, male or female," says Jill. "We're really all the same. I think if we found life on other planets, we'd see ourselves as just human. And that would be a very good thing."

Jill sits down and glances at the information displayed on the computer monitors. The computers do much of the work automatically. The search would be impossible without their help. Computers never daydream about their favorite movie, think about a dish of ice cream, or get bored. They quietly examine the stars, one by one.

Tonight Jill and her team are concerned because they can't locate the faint signal of *Pioneer 10*. Jill thinks that *Pioneer 10* might have finally stopped transmitting or that its antenna is no longer pointing toward Earth.

"If we can use our equipment to find the spacecraft, which is now so far away that it moves in the sky the way distant stars do, it shows that everything is working," says Jill. "It's really a check that everything is A-OK."

As the computer finishes examining each star, Jill makes a note in the log. The log gives a quick overview of the night's observations. Jill takes special care to record anything out of the ordinary, such as equipment problems, power surges, or unusual signals. At twelve-thirty A.M., she discovers something interesting. She stops writing and stares at the monitor.

A signal seems to be coming from star number HD214850AB, a star very much like our own sun. Jill and Seth watch while

Wherever people do SETI observations, the Flag of Earth is flown. James Cadle, an Illinois farmer, designed this flag in 1970 to represent all the citizens of Earth. The yellow, blue, and white circles stand for the sun, the earth, and the moon. SETI astronomers have adopted the flag because they want the people of Earth to know that any signal received from space will belong to everyone.

Jill adjusts the strength of the signal coming from the dish so it can be analyzed by SETI's computers. The astronomers call this the patch panel room, because it is full of bits and pieces of electronic equipment used to patch the signal from the dish to the scientist who is studying it.

the telescope is moved slightly to one side of the star. Jill wants to see if the signal goes away when it's not pointing at the star.

Jill concentrates all her attention on the incoming data. Christopher Columbus, scanning the horizon for signs of the New World, might have worn a similar expression.

"So far this is looking good," says Seth, "but I'm not ready to call my mom yet."

In a few minutes, a thin white line reappears on the monitor. Seth's mom will have to wait. It's not a hit after all. The signal is coming from a satellite or another local source. The only life that Jill and the others have found is—life on Earth.

Everyone relaxes. Someone passes around sandwiches and crackers. Tonight a television crew is on hand to interview Jill while she works. This, too, is part of her job. When she is not at Arecibo, Jill is often asked to give talks to the public to help raise money for SETI. Visitors and journalists who can help spread the word about the exciting work being done here are invited to visit.

"Fundraising has become an important part of my life and one of the reasons I'm on an airplane all the time," she says. "It's so much fun to come here because there's one important job to do and everything else comes second."

The rest of Jill's watch is uneventful. She chats with the visitors and makes occasional notes in the log. Someone starts asking rock 'n' roll trivia questions, and everyone laughs.

Jill likes to relax on the porch of her cabin, listening to the sounds of the rainforest.

When her shift ends at dawn, Jill often goes for a jog around the telescope. Then she returns to her cabin to read, write papers for scientific journals, and answer the many e-mail messages she gets from scientists, journalists, and even children.

The scientists' quarters are at the top of a hill surrounded by forest. The quarters look like army barracks—only no one here is doing pushups. Jill's cabin contains a bedroom, bathroom, and small kitchenette. Inside, papers and a laptop are piled on a built-in desk in the bedroom. A couple of lizards cling to the barren walls, acting as tiny bug-catchers.

Almost every afternoon, lightning flickers and thunder booms, trailing off into a low, distant rumble. When it rains, Jill relaxes on the porch, enjoying the sky, the forest, and the scent of the wet earth.

For dinner, Jill sometimes cooks up an omelet with cheese, green chiles, and mushrooms. Or she might join some of the other scientists for a sandwich or a salad at the observatory cafeteria.

Geckos and tiny tree frogs called *coqui* are sometimes cabin companions.

The scientists often dine on one of the outdoor picnic tables. Mosquitoes and flies usually thrive in a tropical climate, but they are not a problem here because of the hungry hordes of lizards and tree frogs that blanket the island. The tree frogs, called *coqui*, hide themselves so completely that many Puerto Ricans have never actually seen one. But everyone has heard them.

"If you're here at night, walking from the observatory back up to your room, there's a symphony," says Jill. "The little tree frogs go, 'Coqui! Coqui! Coqui!' You know you're in Puerto Rico when you hear that sound."

Bedtime for Jill is four in the afternoon. At midnight,

she's back in the control room—right where she wants to be. Jill has devoted her life to looking for signals from space. And she believes she has the best job in the world.

"She's a fine leader and can do absolutely anything," says Kent Cullers, SETI's Research and Development manager. "I know she can't be working on SETI twenty-four hours a day, but it seems she is."

Jill knows that she might not live to see humans make contact with extraterrestrials, but she believes it will happen eventually. Some scientists argue that humans are the only intelligent beings in the universe. Jill and the others on the SETI team don't agree.

"I think that there might be other life in our galaxy because of two numbers—a very small number and a very large number," says Jill. "The small number is the short time it took for life to evolve after there was liquid water on our planet. Life happened as soon as it could."

"The large number tells us how many stars there are in our galaxy—about 400 billion. Perhaps one tenth of them are very much like our own sun. And the universe contains another 100 billion galaxies beyond our own Milky Way. I suspect that there are lots of other places where conditions would be suitable for life."

Jill does not know who or what might be sending signals our way. She has no picture in her mind of what extraterrestrials might look like.

"Some really bizarre creatures have evolved here on Earth,"

Early evening is a good time to catch up on e-mail correspondence with friends and scientists around the world.

Nobody knows what extraterrestrial life may look like. Even on Earth, evolution has produced an incredible variety of animal forms.

she says. "We know that certain microbes can survive in scalding water. Other creatures survive without water at all. Some creatures live inside frozen rocks in Antarctica. Nature has done some incredible things, and alien life could be different from anything we know."

What kind of signals should scientists look for? Ordinary light cannot penetrate the huge clouds of dust and gas that drift through space. But another kind of electromagnetic radiation—radio waves—could carry messages. These waves pass easily through dust and gas.

Catwalks give access to the platform, a huge superstructure that holds the Gregorian dome and other equipment, suspended hundreds of feet above the dish.

CHAPTER TWO
LISTENING TO THE STARS

AS THE sun rises in the east, Jill Tarter surveys the tropical forest from a cat-walk on the platform of the Arecibo telescope. Rolling hills of green jungle surround the telescope on all sides. Mist hugs the floors of the valleys, and little birds perch on the steel cables that support the platform.

The cables, eighteen in number, are attached to three concrete towers, all at the same height. Tension in the cables is constantly monitored to keep the platform stable and secure.

"The Arecibo telescope is the biggest telescope in the world," says Jill. "It allows us to find the faintest signals. Working with this telescope is a wonderful experience— a little like being at the controls of a gigantic spaceship."

Each year, astronomers come from all over the world to use this powerful telescope—an instrument that can see through clouds, rain, and even thunderstorms. They come to hear the murmurings of stars, the clicks of pulsars, or the hum of distant galaxies. Others come to listen to the heartbeat of quasars and other objects at the very edge of the universe.

Because so many astronomers want to use the telescope, Jill and her team must limit their search to forty days per year—twenty days in the fall and twenty days in the spring.

It is the size of the dish that makes the Arecibo Observatory useful to astronomers. The telescope is so large that it can collect extremely weak radio waves coming from outer space. If there were Martians with cell phones, their calls could be detected.

Radio waves are oscillations that travel through space at the speed of light. If a stone is dropped into a pond, ripples will move away from the center and make small objects on the water bob up and down as they pass by. Radio waves, too, spread out from a source in all directions, but at a rate much faster than ripples on a pond. They move at approximately 186,000 miles (300,000 kilometers) per second.

The dish at Arecibo receives these waves and reflects them upward 450 feet (137 meters) to the six-story-high Gregorian dome, named after James Gregory, who invented the modern reflector telescope. Inside the dome, the waves are focused by metallic mirrors and sent to receivers. Information from the receivers then travels to computers, where it is analyzed.

The Project Phoenix team has its own special equipment that processes information from the telescope. The thirty-ton mobile research facility, or MRF, contains sensitive computer chips and circuit boards that allow the scientists to search for radio signals quickly and efficiently. When the team leaves Arecibo, the MRF is stored next to the telescope control room.

Jill and her team begin each twenty-day observation period by testing the MRF, which has not been used for six months. The tropical heat and the salty air can create rust and other problems.

If all the equipment is working properly, the search begins. The computers select a star similar in size and age to our own sun—not too hot, not too cool, not too big,

FACING PAGE: Most people are amazed when they first see the size of the telescope's dish. The 1000-foot (305-meter) aluminum dish covers an area the size of twenty-six football fields. It would take 10 billion bowls of cereal to fill it to the brim.

The Gregorian dome (*right*), attached underneath
the platform (*facing page*), collects the radio waves
reflected from the dish before they are sent to the
computers to be analyzed.

and not too young. The scientists have programmed the computers to give preference
to stars that are in front of other stars so that more than one can be searched at a time.

Then the computers scan the star, listening to a chunk of 56 million channels in
the microwave portion of the radio spectrum. It's a little like pushing the search or
scan button on a car radio to find a station—in this case, an extraterrestrial station.
If no signal is found, the computers move to a higher frequency and examine another
56 million channels. When a total of 2 billion channels have been searched—or when
the star has set or moved out of range of the telescope—another target is selected.

"The computers swallow a big chunk of radio information," says Jill. "They slice it up into tiny little channels, kind of like slicing a salami. They carefully analyze every single piece to see if there's a pattern."

The pattern Jill is looking for is a narrow-band signal, one limited to a small part of the radio spectrum. If the computers detect a narrow-band signal coming from a certain region, they tell a second radio telescope at Jodrell Bank, England, to scan the same part of the sky. A false signal from a nearby source will not be seen by the second telescope.

If the second telescope locates the target signal, the computers at Arecibo make one last test. They order the Arecibo telescope to move away from the star and point to an empty patch of sky. If the signal disappears, it probably is coming from that star. The telescope then tracks the star again and tries to reacquire the signal. If the signal passes all these tests, the computers are programmed to dial cell phones and pagers and broadcast a message, notifying everyone on the SETI team that something interesting has been found. The SETI scientists keep a bottle of champagne on hand to celebrate this exciting event if it should occur. So far, no Arecibo signals have passed all these tests.

False signals occur once or twice a night at Arecibo. Radiation bouncing off the dome or cables of the telescope is sometimes picked up by the receivers, and this kind of radiation can appear to be coming from space, when it is actually produced by a nearby source.

Radio information from the telescope is processed by a high-speed computer in the Mobile Research Facility, which breaks it into 56 million channels and searches each one for a signal.

The airwaves are buzzing with narrow-band signals. Microwave ovens, garage door openers, satellites, and even sparkplugs can cause interference that looks like the real thing to astronomers.

"A few years ago, the folks here at Arecibo looked out from the platform and saw a newly erected TV transmitter on a nearby mountain," says Jill. "The astronomers here had to work with that television station to provide a huge amount of shielding to keep stray TV emissions from getting into the telescope."

When the Project Phoenix astronomers begin their twenty-day observation period, they map all current sources of interference. They teach the computer to recognize and screen out these sources. Some parts of the spectrum contain so much interference that they have to be skipped, and not all sources can be discovered and accounted for. A false alarm can cause real mischief.

In June 1997, Project Phoenix was using a 140-foot telescope in West Virginia and a second telescope in Georgia to check the results. Unfortunately, the second telescope was hit by lightning and couldn't be repaired for a few days.

"So we detected a signal one morning," recalls Jill. "We went off source. The signal went away. We came back on source, and it was there. We really started to get excited. We spent hours doing this. Going off source in all different directions and coming back on. Each time the signal was still there.

"I was scheduled to go home, to get on a plane that afternoon and leave. I called the office and said, 'I'm not going to go. I won't be in the office tomorrow because something interesting is happening.'"

That little piece of news soon spread around the country.

"Seth was sitting in his office back in Mountain View, California," Jill remembers. "He gets a call from a reporter at the *New York Times*, saying, 'I hear you've got an interesting signal.'"

It took Jill and the others a day to realize that the telescope had picked up SOHO, a satellite that orbits the sun rather than Earth. It was a false alarm.

Underneath the huge dish, workers have to trim back lush ferns, begonias, and wild orchids to keep them from interfering with the reflecting surface.

SETI astronomers have detected thousands of narrow-band signals, but each has been found to be caused by interference. No signal has passed the tests that would identify it as belonging to an extraterrestrial intelligence—at least, not yet.

Jill laughs. "It fooled us all for a while," she says. "If the telescope in Georgia had been working, we would have thrown out this signal right away."

But an important lesson can be learned from this experience. Jill believes that news of contact with extraterrestrials could never be hidden from the public.

People often ask if SETI astronomers have ever picked up a signal that might have been real. The answer is no. But a few mysterious signals have caused excitement.

The best-known of these is the "Wow!" signal detected by Ohio State University volunteer Jerry Ehman. On August 15, 1977, Ehman was looking at the computer printouts from the Ohio State telescope when he saw something unusual.

What he saw was a signal thirty times stronger than the background radio noise from space. In addition, the signal was coming from a special radio channel that isn't used by satellites, airports, radar systems, or radio and television stations.

Jerry Ehman was so impressed with the signal that he wrote "Wow!" on the computer paper in red ink. Unfortunately, this signal was never seen again.

"Even if intelligent beings were sending a signal, they'd do it far more than once," says Dr. Ehman, who is still involved with SETI. "We still don't know what it was, and we probably never will." Most scientists agree.

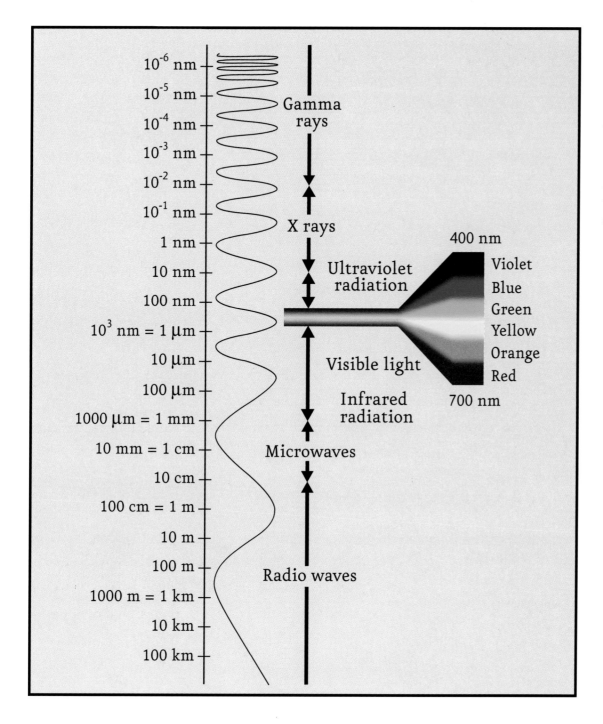

Many objects in space emit a stream of energy (consisting of electric and magnetic fields) traveling in a wavelike pattern at the speed of light. These waves are classified according to their wavelength, and include gamma rays, x-rays, ultraviolet and visible light waves, infrared waves, microwaves, and radio waves. The entire range of waves is called the electromagnetic spectrum. SETI scientists look for signals primarily in the microwave portion of the spectrum. (Microwaves have a wavelength of one millimeter to thirty centimeters.)

CHAPTER THREE
A GIRL ENGINEER

Jill as a child.

WHEN JILL Cornell Tarter was a child, she loved Buck Rogers and Flash Gordon movies. Flash and his crew fought Ming the Merciless on the planet Mongo, blasting off toward the stars in a backyard-built spaceship.

"I don't remember the women," says Jill. "I just wanted to be the guy driving the tin can. That was fun. That was adventure."

Jill also liked to fix things. "I'd take apart a radio or a clock, and when I put it back together, there would be a few bits and pieces left over," she says. "Then I'd say, 'Oops! Where did these come from?' And, of course, the radio or clock was *really* broken after that."

Jill describes herself as a tomboy who hated to wear dresses. Born January 16, 1944, in Eastchester, New York, Jill was the only child of Richard and Betty Cornell. Jill's father was the center of her universe. He took her on weekend camping trips as soon as she could braid her own hair. The two of them hiked and fished in the Catskill Mountains in upstate New York.

"My dad wanted a son," she says, "and I was what he got."

She also remembers taking long walks along a Florida beach with her father while gazing up at the night sky. To Jill, the stars seemed like tiny beacons of light in a vast universe.

She would think, *Those stars are somebody else's suns, and surely somebody out there is looking down at us. How amazing to think that someone or something could be wondering about us, just as we're looking at them.*

When Jill was about eight, her father had a serious conversation with her. He told her that she should spend more time with her mother, learning how to be a young lady instead of spending each weekend with him in the woods.

"I thought that was the most unreasonable thing that anyone had ever said to me," recalls Jill. "I was told that the world was divided into male or female. You had to live in one half and you couldn't live in the other. I just couldn't understand why I couldn't do both."

Soon after that conversation, Jill told her father that she wanted to be an engineer. She had no idea what engineers did. But she knew that most engineers were men, not women. This time, Jill's father said he would support her. He told her that she could

LEFT: Jill loved to go hiking and fishing with her father.
RIGHT: As a girl, Jill was curious about the natural world and came to appreciate and respect its many wonderful creatures.

Jill, second from left, at summer camp.

be anything she wanted to be, if she worked hard enough.

When Jill was twelve, her father died. After that, the idea of becoming an engineer became fixed in her mind. She was determined to prove she could succeed—for her dad.

In high school, Jill wanted to take shop class, since she had always enjoyed building things with her hands. But Jill's high school counselor told her that girls had to take home economics. Jill had an answer for that. First she took home economics—and then she took shop.

"Fortunately, my mom was willing to back me up all the way," says Jill. "I learned that the way to get what you want is to do the extra work. And then people can't say no."

Jill was an excellent student. Her high school physics teacher, known as "Doc," became a second father to her. He worked with Jill and encouraged her interest in science.

A fad was sweeping through Jill's high school. The girls in her class had started wearing chicken wishbones on chains around their necks. Jill wanted to make her wishbone special, so she decided to coat it with silver. Doc agreed to help.

"We worked and worked on that project," she recalls. "Doc didn't know how to do it, either." But they eventually figured it out. By rubbing graphite onto the wishbone, they finally got it to plate.

Jill had other interests besides science. When Doc arranged to have her go to a special Saturday science program at Columbia University, she turned it down. She was the head drum majorette and had to attend the Saturday football games.

Still determined to be an engineer, Jill prepared to go to college. She knew of a special scholarship available to the descendants of Ezra Cornell, the man who had founded Cornell University. Jill, a descendant of Ezra Cornell's half-brother, decided to apply.

"We just didn't have a lot of money," she says. "We wrote to Cornell University and asked. And there was a very interesting reply. It said, well, yes, there was such a thing, but it was only for male descendants. I couldn't apply."

"It was the early sixties," she says. "And I thought, Oh well, that's the way things are."

But two days later, Jill received news that she had been granted a full scholarship to Cornell from Procter & Gamble. That plus a Regents scholarship from the state of New York paid for her education.

At Cornell, she was the only woman among three hundred male engineering students. It wasn't always easy being the only

Jill's daughter, Shana, has come to appreciate her mother's amazing career.

The well-known astronomer Carl Sagan, sixth from the left, appears to the left of Jill in this picture. Carl Sagan wrote the book *Contact*, a novel based loosely on Jill's life and career.

female engineer. Jill was locked in the women's dormitory every night and had to do all the homework assignments by herself. The male students, who were together in the men's dormitory, shared the homework.

"As a result, I got a better education than the men did," says Jill.

Jill finished the five-year engineering program in four years. In the summer of her junior year, she got married and soon had a daughter, Shana. After graduation, Jill decided to change fields. She had good analytical and problem-solving skills, but engineering no longer interested her.

After taking a class on star formation, Jill decided that astronomers were working on the kinds of problems she wanted to solve. Eventually Jill focused her efforts on SETI and has received many awards and honors for her work.

But for years, Jill's daughter was unimpressed with her mother's success. When Shana was asked to list her mother's occupation on school forms, she wrote "looks for little green men."

In part, Carl Sagan, the author and astronomer, used Jill as the model for Ellie Arroway when he wrote the book *Contact*. "In 1985 Carl sent me a copy of the book and I was stunned when I read it," says Jill. "It was so like me."

Jodie Foster, who played Ellie in the movie, spent time with Jill at Arecibo, where some of the scenes in the film were shot. The special effects crew came to the SETI Institute to study the clothes, the computer equipment, and even the coffee cups used by the astronomers. Jill appreciates the interest sparked by the movie because it's brought attention to SETI.

Today Jill has a happy family life as well as a successful career. She is married to Jack Welch, who holds the only endowed University Chair for SETI at UC Berkeley. Both like dancing. They also own a small aircraft, a Cessna 210 that Jill loves to fly.

Jill and her husband, Jack, share many interests, including a love of the outdoors.

Jill is good with a sewing machine, and she enjoys making shirts for her husband. They sometimes do small construction projects together. Recently she and Jack built a cover for a pool table so they could play Ping-Pong on the top. But the main thing the couple shares is a commitment to SETI.

"We're both driven by our curiosity," says Jill. "We're doing what we love."

CHAPTER FOUR
PLANETS AND MOONS

AS DIRECTOR of SETI Research, Jill keeps track of everything that goes on. When she is not on a plane or giving a speech, she can be found in her office in Mountain View, California. Various awards and medals are on display, as well as family photos. Along with the space-related pictures and posters are mementos of Jill's many travels—on Earth, that is.

You can hear the enthusiasm in Jill's voice when she mentions the exciting new developments in her field. The recent discovery of extrasolar planets, those that orbit other stars, is of special interest to SETI scientists.

Astronomers can't actually see these extrasolar planets. But they can measure a slight wobble in the stars that the planets orbit. The wobble is caused by gravity tugging on a star as a planet moves around it. Only the largest planets can be detected using this method. These large planets are probably made up of swirling clouds of hydrogen and helium, and most astronomers think that they cannot support life.

"When astronomers discover planets around a star, we give that star more priority and we try to observe it as soon as we can," says Peter Backus.

Jill works on a stack of paperwork in her office at the SETI Institute in Mountain View, California.

Awards and travel mementos cover the walls and shelves of Jill's office.

Many scientists believe that water is also necessary for life to evolve. If a planet is too close to its star, any water on it would boil away. And if it's too far away, the water would freeze. So they look for small, Earth-like planets that are not too close or too far away from the stars they orbit.

A space telescope equipped with a photometer, an instrument that measures the intensity of light, can find stars that dim and brighten very slightly at regular intervals. If the alignment is just right, a planet revolving around a star can seem to disappear behind it. At other times, it will pass in front of the star, blocking a tiny portion of the light. If the measurements are precise enough, even small planets can be detected in this way.

"With a space telescope, you can look at one hundred thousand stars continuously over a period of several years," says Jill. "Occasionally you'll get a little blip when a planet is passing in front of a certain star. Then the planet will come around again and you'll get a second blip. If you can predict when the blip will come again and detect it on schedule, you will know that you have discovered a planet and not a flickering star."

The European Space Agency has plans to launch the Darwin Space Infrared Interferometer in 2015. This telescope, forty times larger than the Hubble Space Telescope, will collect infrared heat rather than visible light. NASA has plans for a similar instrument called the Terrestrial Planet Finder (TPF). These two telescopes will search for Earth-like planets and try

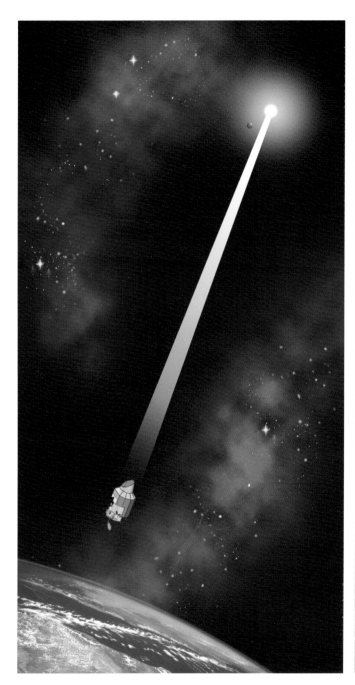

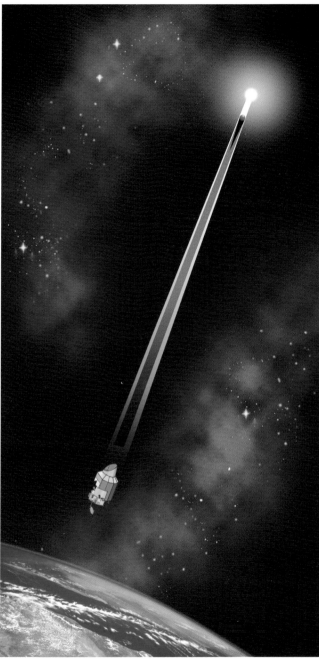

A satellite fitted with a photometer looks for planets by studying the change in light received from stars. If a planet passes in front of a star, the light from that star will dim very slightly. By measuring this very accurately, a photometer should even be able to detect planets as small as Earth.

Many scientists wonder if life might have evolved on Mars. Early in its history, Mars probably had a wetter, warmer, and thicker atmosphere than it has today.

to detect water and oxygen, a byproduct of life, in the atmospheres of any planets they find.

"When you are trying to see a small planet that's going around a very bright star, it's like trying to see a firefly that's perched on the edge of some big spotlight miles away," says Jill. "When viewed through an optical telescope, a planet is a billion times fainter than its star. But when viewed in infrared, it's only a million times fainter."

While some scientists are reaching out to the stars, others are looking closer to home. They are looking for life on the planets and moons in our own solar system. The red planet, Mars, has often been thought of as a possible home for alien life.

In 1971, the spacecraft *Mariner 9* came within 1,025 miles of Mars and sent back detailed pictures of an astounding world. Wild dust storms raged across the Martian surface, and sand dunes shifted as winds piled them here and there. Mars is a planet of huge volcanoes, deep canyons, and old riverbeds. The temperature at the surface of Mars seldom rises above the freezing point of water. Was life possible in such a place?

In 1976, two NASA spacecraft, the *Viking Landers*, settled on the rust-colored surface of Mars and performed experiments designed to answer this question. The experiments found nothing, not even microbes. Most scientists concluded that Mars was a dead planet.

But new evidence has challenged those findings. Life, as we know it, can exist on Earth because there is water, and signs of liquid water can be seen on Mars. Many researchers believe that Mars was once warmer and wetter than it is today. It may be that most of the water on Mars escaped into space long ago. Or it may be that a layer of water still exists in a frozen state under the surface and seeps upward from time to time. Could this water contain microscopic life?

An even more exciting claim involves a greenish-gray rock about the size of a potato found in Antarctica in 1984. In 1993, scientists realized that the rock, a meteorite, probably came from Mars. How did they know this? Gases trapped in the rock closely matched the gases that the *Viking Landers* had measured on Mars in 1976.

Then the scientists found something even more amazing. Using lasers and high-powered microscopes, they found evidence that the rock had been submerged in water when Mars was still warm and wet—four and a half billion years ago. Tiny tubelike forms could be seen through the microscopes. These forms looked very much like the fossils of microorganisms on Earth.

Many researchers are not convinced that the remains of ancient, microscopic life on Mars have been found—and the debate continues. But most agree that if life could arise separately on two different planets, Earth and Mars, it probably exists on many other worlds as well.

"There's an enormous amount of interest in this question of life on Mars," says Jill. "It continues to be an open issue."

While Mars is cold, Europa, one of Jupiter's moons, is even

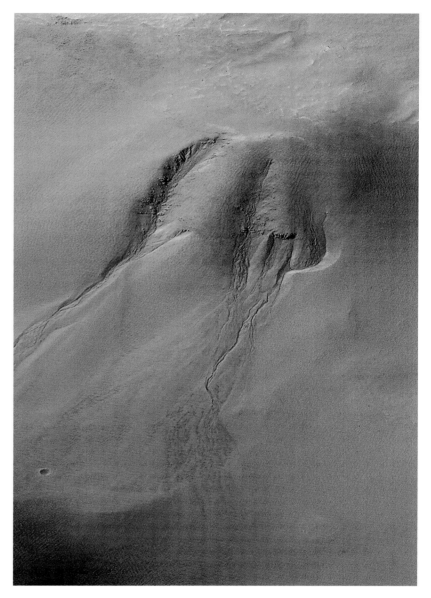

Photographs taken by the Mars Global Surveyor in 1999 show evidence of recent channeling and erosion that might be caused by liquid water seeping out from frozen layers buried underneath. Could simple life still survive beneath the Martian surface? (Courtesy of NASA/JPL/Malin Space Science Systems)

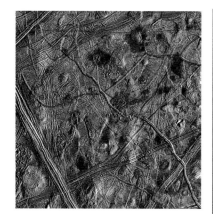

Europa, one of Jupiter's moons, may have a liquid-water ocean beneath its fractured, frozen surface.

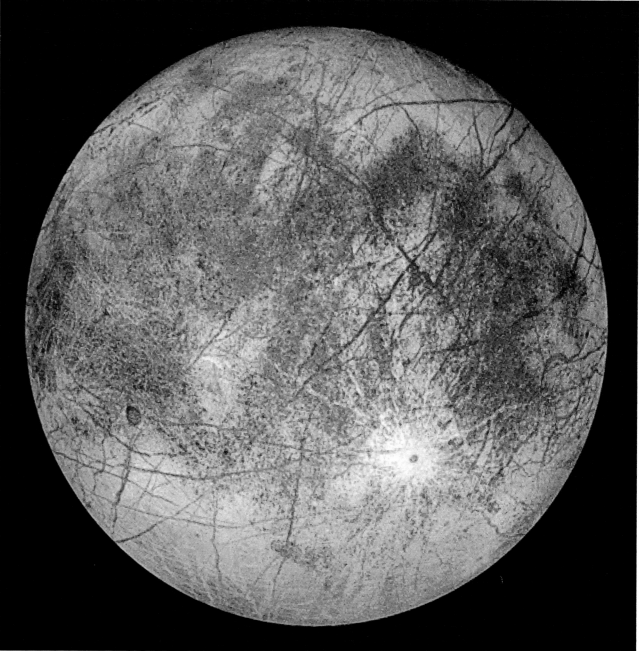

colder. Surprisingly, scientists think that Europa—and possibly Callisto and Ganymede, two other moons of Jupiter—might harbor life.

Europa is the sixth largest moon in the solar system. Seen from space, it appears to be crisscrossed with lines that make it look like a cracked egg. The lines are thought to be fractures in Europa's thick, icy crust caused by water welling up from below. Scientists believe that a huge ocean of liquid water, bigger than the Atlantic and Pacific oceans combined, may lie beneath Europa's surface. Life *might* be able to exist there.

Living on the surface of Europa would be something like living on an iceberg in the Arctic Ocean with almost no sunlight or air. Even a polar bear wearing a ski parka wouldn't want to live in a place where the temperature is more than 130 Fahrenheit degrees (70 Celsius degrees) lower than in Vostok, Antarctica, the coldest place on Earth.

Europa is engaged in a gravitational tug-of-war with Jupiter and two other moons, Io and Ganymede. The changing tidal pull, which alternately stretches and squeezes Europa, might heat the water underneath the ice and keep the huge ocean from freezing. Do tiny microbes swim in the inky depths of Europa's liquid ocean?

"Chris Chyba, who holds the Carl Sagan Chair at the SETI Institute, is very interested in Europa," says Jill. "There are frozen lakes in the Dry Valleys of Antarctica. But if you dive under the ice, you'll find a mat of living microbes. It's quite possible that life is present on Europa. If it's true, we'd very much like to get under that ice."

"If we find a second example of life in our own solar system, it would mean that life is absolutely everywhere," says Jill. "Number two is really important."

Scientists at the SETI Institute have been comparing photographs of Europa taken at different times to look for changes in its cracked surface, which would suggest the movement of liquid water beneath.

CHAPTER FIVE
THINKING BIG

NOBODY KNOWS when, or if, the SETI team will find an extraterrestrial radio signal. At the present time, Project Phoenix is working on a list of 1,000 sunlike stars, searching them one by one. To increase the odds of success, the SETI Institute, in partnership with the University of California at Berkeley, is building its own telescope, the Allen Telescope Array, to be completed in 2005.

"The target list will be increased to 100,000 stars," says Jill. "The Allen Telescope will speed up our search and make it about one hundred times faster."

Older radio telescopes, like the one at Arecibo, are huge, single dishes. The Allen Telescope Array will consist of hundreds of small dishes standing together in a field. The dishes (6 meters, or 19.7 feet, in diameter) will be linked by computers, and together they will have more power than any single dish.

The telescope, to be located in a "radio-quiet" area near Mount Lassen in Northern California, will cost $26 million to build. It will search the sky twenty-four hours a day, seven days a week, allowing the SETI scientists twenty times as much observing time as they now have at Arecibo.

"Forty nights a year at Arecibo is a huge amount of time," says Jill. "But it's not as much as we'd like. The array will allow us to point the telescope at a number of different stars at the same time. And we will be able to process more of the radio spectrum than we can now."

A smaller version of the Allen Telescope Array is already up and working near the UC Berkeley Leuchner Observatory. Using the model, scientists can experiment with different ways of controlling the dishes and hooking them together to avoid interference from satellites.

More dishes can be added to the telescope, so it could eventually become the largest radio telescope in the world. Other radio astronomers will be able to study galaxies, neutron stars, and objects that interest them at the same time SETI scientists use the telescope to examine target stars.

"It's a win-win situation for everyone," says Jill.

Astronomers sometimes say that what SETI does is like searching for a needle in a haystack. "Up until now, SETI has been using a teaspoon to go through that hay," says Seth. "The new Allen telescope will be more like a shovel."

SETI scientists are beginning to think about new methods of doing SETI searches. One possibility is to scan the universe for pulses of laser light. An amateur astronomer, Dr. Stuart Kingsley of Columbus, Ohio, has used a ten-inch optical telescope in his backyard to search for brief pulses of a laser beam that might

Several small dishes are tested near Berkeley to help astronomers choose a final design for the Allen Telescope Array. The laptop shows an artist's impression of how the final array might look with hundreds of dishes working together.

A telescope made up of many small dishes linked together needs a complex control system. This worker at the University of California's Radio Astronomy Laboratory is helping to design a system for the Allen Telescope Array.

be directed at Earth. New programs at UC Santa Cruz, UC Berkeley, and Harvard University are examining nearby stars for laser signals. If the stars are close to Earth, dust and gas won't absorb the signals.

The SETI Institute astronomers are also asking the question, What happens if we make contact? In 1989, Jill, Michael Michaud, and others prepared a plan of action in case a signal is found. All major SETI researchers have agreed to abide by the plan. After the signal is verified as extraterrestrial, the researchers will notify other astronomers, the government, and the public. If the signal is real, the world will know right away. There will be no secrecy.

"Science works very slowly, and journalists will probably be pressing for answers

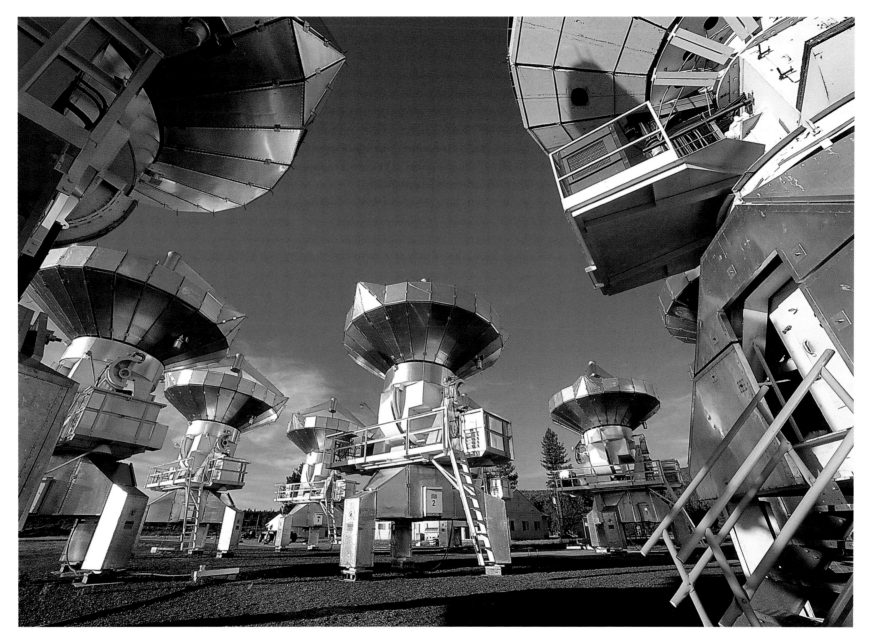

Scientists believe that combining the power of small dishes, like this dish array currently in use at the Mt. Lassen site, is the best way to build the next generation of radio telescopes. Hundreds of linked units working together will increase the effectiveness of the Allen Telescope Array.

In 1974 the Arecibo telescope was used to transmit a message to a star cluster across the galaxy. It included symbols representing a human and the solar system. An extraterrestrial civilization with a receiving telescope the same size as the Arecibo dish would be able to detect the signal—but nobody's expecting a reply soon. It will take 21,000 years for the signal to reach its destination, and as long again for a reply to return.

much more quickly than we'll be able to give them," says Doug Vakoch, Project Phoenix social scientist. "One of the big questions we'll need to ask is, Should we reply to the signal? I propose we actually draft some messages right now. If we spend the next fifty or one hundred years doing that, it would be all to the good."

A program launched in 1999, SETI@home, allows anyone with a computer and an Internet connection to join the search. SETI@home volunteers download a free screen saver program. Screen savers are programs that produce moving images on the screen of a computer when it is idle. Once installed on a computer, the program retrieves a

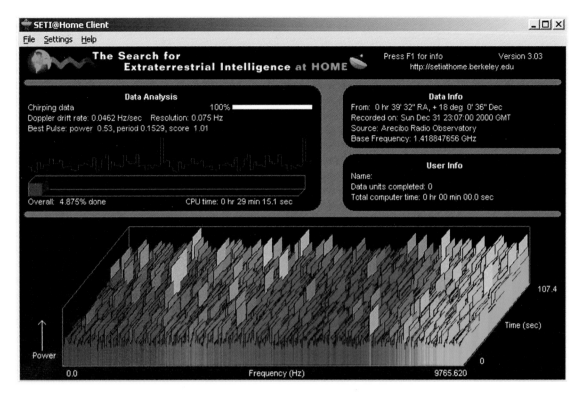

chunk of data from Arecibo, analyzes it, and returns the results to a group of scientists at UC Berkeley.

The Berkeley scientists are conducting a type of SETI search called an all-sky survey. Instead of looking closely at one star at a time as Project Phoenix astronomers do, the Berkeley scientists look at a much larger area and scan it at a faster rate.

"The piece of the sky that is looked at moves through the beam of the telescope in twelve seconds," says Jill. "That's not a lot of time. Some of the data gets put onto a large server and cut into little pieces and shipped out, all over the world, to individuals and groups that are running the SETI@home program. The computers can look for patterns that the system doesn't have time to analyze."

Whenever a volunteer's computer is idle, the data is scanned. Instead of showing pictures of monsters or cute goldfish, the screen saver displays a graphic of the data. Strong signals look like tall redwoods in a grassy field. Most of these are caused by interference from planes or satellites, picked up when the data was gathered. But a place in the history books is reserved for the person whose computer records the first signal from extraterrestrials.

Today more than 3 million people in 226 countries—schoolchildren, retirees, doctors, lawyers, and housewives—use SETI@home. Working together, these millions of computers are twice as powerful as the brainiest supercomputer on Earth. The success of SETI@home shows that many people all over the world share Jill's passion.

"I get to work on something that's incredibly important and could have a large impact on the world," says Jill. "I'm fortunate to be able to do something I really love. I say I'm fortunate, but it isn't just by accident. If I hadn't had a good education, if I hadn't gone to the university, if I didn't have an advanced degree, I couldn't do this job, which requires a lot of training."

Jill enjoys learning something new every day. She doesn't wake up in the morning thinking she is about to find a signal. But she does wake up thinking about how to make the search better. There is talk of putting a telescope on the far side of the moon, the only place where there is no radio interference from Earth. If that should happen, Jill would like to go.

"There hasn't been a woman on the moon yet," she says with a smile.

Jill is not discouraged by the lack of a signal so far.
The universe is vast, and the places to look for
extraterrestrial life are almost infinite.

Good Planets Are Hard To Find

Searching for Alien Life: Is Anyone Out There? by Dennis Brindell Fradin (New York: Twenty-First Century, 1997) is written for young adults and discusses the history of SETI searches, contact with extraterrestrials, and the feasibility of interstellar travel.

Life in the Universe Curriculum, for grades 3 through 9. Available from the SETI Institute online gift shop (store.yahoo.com/seti-store), this book discusses evolution, planetary systems, and how life might evolve on other worlds.

Is Anybody Out There? by Heather Couper and Nigel Henbest (New York: DK Publishing, 1998) presents brief facts about UFOs, the solar system, the search for alien life, and other related topics.

Sharing the Universe: Perspectives on Extraterrestrial Life by Seth Shostak (Berkeley, Calif.: Berkeley Hills Books, 1998) is written for adults by a member of the SETI Institute, but it is accessible to some young readers, containing entertaining and engaging information on the search for intelligent extraterrestrials.

The Universe by Seymour Simon (New York: William Morrow, 1998) takes readers on a quick tour of the universe.

Eyewitness: Astronomy by Kristen Lippincott (New York: DK Publishing, 2000) covers the history of astronomy, including a discussion of sundials, planets, space exploration, and black holes.

WEB SITES FOR KIDS

SETI@HOME

www.setiathome.ssl.berkeley.edu

Download a special screen saver and help the SETI scientists.

THE SETI INSTITUTE ONLINE

www.seti-inst.edu

Includes frequently asked questions about SETI, SETI@Arecibo, teachers' materials, and a "Who's Out There?" interactive game for kids.

AN ASTRONOMY COURSE FOR STUDENTS USING THE INTERNET

www.darkskyinstitute.org/astronomy.html

A course for middle and high school students with information on the moon, the sun, the stars, galaxies, quasars, nebulae, the Big Bang, and much more.

ASTRONOMY AND SPACE FOR KIDS

www.kidinfo.com/science/astronomy.html

Take a tour of the solar system, ask an astronomer questions, and learn about black holes, comets, constellations, eclipses, and phases of the moon. For elementary students.

GLOSSARY

Jill loves the varieties of bananas and other tropical fruit in Puerto Rico.

ANTENNA —the part of a radio telescope that collects or receives radio waves.

ARRAY —a system of individual radio-wave detectors that feed their signals into a common receiver.

ASTROPHYSICIST —a scientist who studies the physical features of stars, planets, and other astronomical bodies.

CHANNEL —a narrow band of frequencies within the radio spectrum.

DISH —the bowl-shaped part of a radio telescope used to collect and focus radio waves from outer space.

DRY VALLEYS —an extremely cold, desert region of Antarctica that gets no snowfall but contains lakes formed from melting glaciers.

ELECTROMAGNETIC RADIATION —a term that describes a continuous spectrum of radiation made up of electrical and magnetic fields. Electromagnetic radiation includes gamma rays, x-rays, ultraviolet and visible light waves, infrared waves, microwaves, and radio waves.

EXTRASOLAR —not belonging to our sun or solar system.

EXTRATERRESTRIAL —a living organism from somewhere other than Earth.

FOSSILS —traces or remains of plant or animal life preserved in rock formations.

GALAXY —a large group of stars, such as our own Milky Way, held together by gravity.

HELIUM —a very light gas; one of the chemical elements.

HYDROGEN —a colorless, flammable gas; the lightest chemical element.

INTERFERENCE —a coming together of two or more radio signals that distorts or prevents reception of the desired signal.

INTERSTELLAR —between or among the stars.

LASER BEAM —an intense beam of light that could be used to communicate with extraterrestrial civilizations.

MICROBES —extremely tiny organisms that can be observed only through a microscope.

MICROORGANISMS —microscopic organisms, such as bacteria, protozoa, or viruses.

MICROWAVE —a type of electromagnetic radiation having wavelengths in the range of one millimeter to thirty centimeters.

NEUTRON STARS —collapsed stars made up of densely packed particles called neutrons.

ORBIT —to travel in a circular path around the sun or a star.

OSCILLATION —a vibration; a moving back and forth between two positions.

PROJECT PHOENIX —a targeted SETI search administered by the SETI Institute that scans individual stars one by one.

QUASAR —a starlike object that is thought to be one of the brightest objects in the universe.

ROTATION —the movement of Earth as it turns on its axis.

SOLAR SYSTEM —the sun and its family of nine planets and their moons.

SPECTRUM —a range of electromagnetic energy that varies in wavelenth, such as the radio spectrum.

UNIVERSE —the totality of everything.

A telescope array has may dishes that work together.

SPECIAL THANKS TO DR. JILL TARTER

Dr. Jill Cornell Tarter is a world leader in the field of SETI (Search for Extraterrestrial Intelligence). She is an astrophysicist and director of SETI Research at the SETI Institute in Mountain View, California, where she holds the Bernard M. Oliver Chair. Dr. Tarter has received many awards and honors, including the Lifetime Achievement Award from Women in Aerospace for her contributions to the fields of exobiology and SETI. She has also received two Public Service Medals from NASA.

Jill rides the cable car to the platform above the Arecibo dish.

✳ NOTE FROM THE AUTHOR

None of the SETI programs mentioned in this book investigates UFO sightings or alien abductions. SETI astronomers search for scientific evidence of extraterrestrial intelligence. Stories of alien abductions and accounts of UFO sightings rely on personal stories, which cannot be scientifically verified.

✳ ACKNOWLEDGMENTS

I am most grateful to Dr. Jill Tarter for sharing her story and giving so generously of her time and scientific expertise. The following members of the SETI team gave me invaluable assistance: Peter R. Backus, D. Kent Cullers, Mike Davis, Jane Jordan, John Ross, Doug Vakoch, and especially Chris Neller and Seth Shostak. A number of people helped me improve this manuscript. These include Dr. Frank J. Spera, Dolly Dickinson, Lowell Dabbs, Andrea Brown, Susie Leska, Carmel Robertson, Mary Hahn, Carol Heyer, Kyle Smith, and Nic Bishop. I would also like to thank Roger Schlueter for giving me advice and encouragement when I most needed it, and June Kelley for transcribing my tapes and commenting on an early draft. Special thanks to my editor, Amy Flynn. —E. J.

I am especially grateful to Jill Tarter for her patience and good humor while being photographed during her busy work schedule. I would also like to thank NASA and the Space Telescope Science Institute (StSci) for the use of their images appearing in this book. These images have been incorporated in digital form within photographs and illustrations on pages 6, 16, 26, 37, 46, and 49. A big thanks to Ellen too, for inviting me. —N.B.

INDEX

Vast regions of hydrogen gas form "nurseries," where new stars are still being born. New life forms, too, may constantly be evolving in the universe. This photograph was produced by the Hubble Space Telescope. The black areas at top right are unscanned parts of the image.